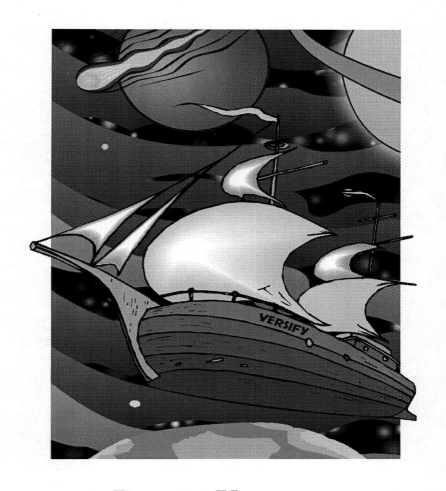

POETIC VOYAGES
WEST NOTTINGHAMSHIRE

Edited by Dave Thomas

First published in Great Britain in 2002 by
YOUNG WRITERS
Remus House,
Coltsfoot Drive,
Peterborough, PE2 9JX
Telephone (01733) 890066

HB ISBN 0 75433 424 4
SB ISBN 0 75433 425 2

FOREWORD

Young Writers was established in 1991 with the aim to promote creative writing in children, to make reading and writing poetry fun.

This year once again, proved to be a tremendous success with over 88,000 entries received nationwide.

The Poetic Voyages competition has shown us the high standard of work and effort that children are capable of today. It is a reflection of the teaching skills in schools, the enthusiasm and creativity they have injected into their pupils shines clearly within this anthology.

The task of selecting poems was therefore a difficult one but nevertheless, an enjoyable experience. We hope you are as pleased with the final selection in *Poetic Voyages West Nottinghamshire* as we are.

CONTENTS

Peafield Lane Primary School

Michael Hale 72

Francesca Withers 72

Lewis Caudwell 72

Jordan Anthony Webster 73

Bethany Ashmore 73

Wendy Mullen 73

Daniel Lilley 74

Matthew Coulton 74

Alex Radford 74

Kieran Morris Owen 75

Thomas Jeffery 75

Heather Allanson 75

Kristy Wright 76

Ben Day 76

Julianne Simmen 76

Marc Preston 77

Naomi Widdowson 77

Scott McGough 77

Hannah Thompson 78

Lucy Shaw 78

Jacob Fogg 79

Richard Delaney 79

Laura Cunnington 80

Lauren Birch 80

Conor Pollard 81

Stephanie Spence 81

Thomas Moore 82

Christian Ashton 82

Christopher Blood 83

Abbie Gray 83

Sarah Beardsley 84

Aaron Magor 84

Hannah Latham 85

Amy Chadwick 85

Ben Dixon 86

Anna Follows 86

Chloe Pettinger 87

Jason Lowe 87

Simon Branch	88
Laura Smith	88
Jodie Rebekah Camm	89
Ricky Machin	89
Leanna Elizabeth Wilson	90
Hollie Munn	90
Katie Hanson	91
Richard Boyfield	91
James Wood	92
Samantha Mawson	92
Scott Noble	93
Rebecca Martindale	93
Steven Woodcock	94
David Hanson	94
Charlotte Field	95
Jonathan Stretton	95
Sarah-Louise Killman	96
Gareth Anderson	96
Charlie Bartlett	97
Sam Moore	97
Josephine Clark	98
Adam Marsden	98
Richard Callaghan	99
Emma Cottrell	99
Sarah Box	100
Natalie Mawson	101
Emma Coppin	102

Saville House School

Rebecca Louise Wass	102
Victoria Bowring	103
Antonios Savva	103
Ellalouise Whetton	104
Hayley Arnold	105
Natalya Baxter	106
Elizabeth Smith	106
Christopher Haslam	107
Matthew Davis	107

The Poems

HOMEWORK

There's things I love,
but school's not one of them.
It's OK, it's not that bad,
it's just homework that makes me mad.
No time to play and things like that.
I get some every single weekend,
which drives me round the bend.
No time to play on computer games,
but now it's just not quite the same.
My parents are there,
they help me out.
So now there's no need to shout . . .

This work's too hard, I need to get out.

Stuart Manning (10)
Blyth Primary School

BIRDS

If only I was a bird
who could sing, dance and play
I'd be so happy I'd fly away
Nuts and bread to eat all day
There's a bird, come sing, dance and play.

I like birds so should you
what joy they bring for me and you.

I'm so near the end, goodbye I say
but birds want to see you
so come sing, dance and play.

Lucy Mastin (10)
Blyth Primary School

MAD ABOUT MUSIC!

Pop, jazz and classical too,
Country, western and blues.
Crotchet, quaver and minim rest,
Everyone knows that music's the best.
Clarinet, bassoon, oboe and flute,
All of these sound with a rooty-toot-toot!
Violin, viola and double bass,
These are all strings and they are ace!
Trumpet, cornet and French horn,
I've loved music since I was born!
Drums bang loudly,
Bells clang soundly,
And cymbals always clash,
But what I am trying to tell you is . . .

I'm mad about music!

Helen Stevenson (10)
Blyth Primary School

FISH

Typical, tropical fish,
Eat them raw or on a dish.

Swimming around all day,
Everything they do they never have to pay.

Dancing having discos,
Eating gravy made from Bisto.

Meeting friends,
Heeling men.

Typical, tropical fish.

Kirsty Dawson (11)
Blyth Primary School

ANIMALS OF THE EARTH

Cheetahs are fast,
Snails are slow,
Dodos are past,
But glow-worms glow.

Tigers go roar,
Mice go squeak,
Hamsters can gnaw,
And slothes just sleep.

Condors can fly,
Ants are slick,
Mayflies die,
And horses are quick.

Frogs go croak,
Whales can sing,
Stoats can stoat,
And wolves go down wind.

Richard Allen (11)
Blyth Primary School

SWANS

Swans are beautiful white too,
I like swans so should you,
Swans fly high up in the sky,
Like a puff of cloud rolling by,
Swans swim on the lake,
What a lovely sight they make.

Emma Whitaker (10)
Blyth Primary School

NATURE

Flowers in the garden
Flowers in the wood
Where a little antelope
Took his first step and stood.

See the little penguin
Learning how to swim
When he saw his mother
He just fell in.

See the little lion cub
Trying to catch some prey
He got so tired he gave up
And he began to play.

See my little hamster
Crawling in my sock
He walked on my model boat
He walked on the dock.

See the little hippo
Splashing in the mud
When he got out
He was covered in suds.

See the little crab
Walking in the sand
Someone picks him up
In their hand.

Danielle Parker (9)
Blyth Primary School

RUNNING!

Running so fast
Then you can't come last

Running so slow
You're going to go low

Running like a jog
Don't trip over a log

Running like a walk
Don't start to talk

Running down a slope
I'm starting to hope

Running on a pin
But I still win.

Charlotte Houghton (10)
Blyth Primary School

MY HOLIDAY

I love going on holiday
I think it's really cool
Sometimes our villa has its own pool

I get a dark suntan
I have lots of fun
Playing around in the hot summer sun

I buy souvenirs
For all my mates
Time to go home, my holiday was great.

Thomas Flint (11)
Blyth Primary School

CRICKET

I went to cricket
With my team
I didn't get a wicket
But that was my dream.

But next time
I'll do better
I'll do fine
But this is just a letter.

My friend's late dad
Didn't make it in time
He drove us mad
But in the end it was fine.

Maisie Hampson (10)
Blyth Primary School

WILD ANIMALS AND PETS

Ducks all have very cute looks,
Cats chase rats,
Dogs go after bones,
Birds fly very high up in the sky,
Bees busy making their honey every day,
they never get a chance to play.
Elephants are very big,
they're too heavy to dance and jig.
Dolphins are the best sea creatures ever,
they're wet whatever the weather.
But ants try to get in your pants.

Lynsey Coleman (10)
Blyth Primary School

WINTER

Winter is my best
better than all the rest
I don't like the summer's glow
I'd rather have the winter's snow

Winter is my favourite
because of the snow
the nice hot fire
and the cold winds that blow

Full of sparkle and pure white
snowflakes dancing in the light
the crunchy feeling under your feet
the snowmen in the gardens, they look so sweet

Winter is my very best
better than all the rest
it's also the time when Santa's here
with presents and sweets and lots of cheer.

Paul Schuller (11)
Blyth Primary School

THE PLANETS

The red planet Mars
Is a wonderful sight
It whirls around with the stars
Shining in the night

The darkest planet Pluto
Is millions of miles away
I wonder if there's life there
And do they have night and day.

Zach Tanner (9)
Blyth Primary School

TRAVELLING TO THE MOON

Travelling to the moon
See a big balloon
Say hello, say goodbye
Travelling to the moon

Travelling to Mars
See lots of stars
They are really bright
Travelling to Mars

Let's go to Earth
It's made of AstroTurf
Play some games, have a good time
Let's go to Earth.

I like the sun
It's better than a bun
It's so amazing
I like the sun.

Karl Snee (9)
Blyth Primary School

TRAVEL

Trains chugging everywhere, there's no time to spare.
Revving engines in the car parks, buses travelling far
Smelly exhausts pollute the air and I don't think it's fair!

Joshua Swannack (10)
Blyth Primary School

SUPERB MOUSE

My name is Superbmouse
I live in a super house

I do as I please
I eat super cheese

I chase rats
And frighten the lives out of the neighbour's cats

Mouse, mouse
My name is Superbmouse.

Timothy Smith (9)
Blyth Primary School

ANIMAL POEM

Monkeys eat
Whales defeat

Lions growl
Wolves prowl

Worms wiggle
Ladybirds jiggle

Apes fight
Crabs bite

Kangaroos leap
But I
Sleep!

Paul Turner (8)
Brookfield Primary School

IN THE JUNGLE

Down in the jungle
Very noisy animals
Roaring and hissing at me
Snakes hissing
Lions roaring
What a noise they make
Walking round
Seeing what I can find
Nothing much
Having lunch
Along came a caterpillar
Munch, munch, munch
Going home
Feeling tired
Just can't wait till I go to
    Bed.

Rebecca Speight (9)
Brookfield Primary School

POLLUTION

Pollution, pollution
What is the solution?
Without any doubt
Health is what it's about

A polluted river
With fumes and gases
Can damage your lungs
With terrible air

All the fumes and gases
Can kill animals in masses
Oil and flammable things
Can cause all sorts of havoc

So please just be careful
So you don't cause anything awful
We need such animals
To keep the world together.

Aden Turner (9)
Brookfield Primary School

WILD POEMS

Elephants charge,
Rhinos barge,

Monkeys munch,
Koalas crunch,

Cheetahs prowl,
Tigers growl,

Penguins wobble,
Lions squabble,

Snakes
Lurk
But people
Work!

Benjamin Chapman (9)
Brookfield Primary School

HALLOWE'EN

Bats are flying,
witches screaming,
chimneys steaming,
children playing.
Bats are flying,
devils fighting,
moonbeams lighting,
trick or treating.
Bats are flying,
vampires slaying,
people praying,
hound dog howling.
Bats are flying.

Lacey Roebuck (8)
Brookfield Primary School

ANIMALS IN THE WILD

In the jungle everywhere,
Creatures lay in their lair.
In the trees, on the ground,
Everywhere not a sound.
Animals in the wild!

In the water crocodiles creep,
In the trees birds sleep.
Running, running cheetahs cheat,
Stamping, stamping elephants beat.
Animals in the wild!

Animals creeping round and round,
Slipping, sliding underground.
Can you hear something?
What is the sound?
Animals in the wild!

Rachael Spiby (9)
Brookfield Primary School

JOBS

My dad's got a job,
He's a businessman,
He's one of the best,
And sells things he can.

My mum's got a job,
She's a dance teacher,
And people who dance
Feel lucky they meet her.

My uncle's got a job,
He's a cook,
His food is tasty,
So I have a look.

My grandma's so old,
She doesn't work,
She's really nice,
And knows where dust lurks.

There's all kinds of jobs,
Like business and cooks,
But I prefer
To read books.

Christopher Thomas (8)
Brookfield Primary School

WINTER

In the long, long winter
I just stood there, stood there in the cold.
I walked and walked,
I was just like steel.
I was as hard as rock,
I was as hard as a boulder,
It's so, so cold.
I was blowing away far, far away,
I go into the snow,
It's squash and squidgy.
Hailstones, hailstones as hard as a rock.
The wind blows and blows
And blows some parts off cliffs.
Icicles hang from cliffs.
Once I nearly blew away,
But I never fear no danger.

Rachael Coppin (8)
Brookfield Primary School

CHRISTMAS

At Christmas my sister got a teddy
She called it Fred and he went to bed
And had some bread at lunch
I got a bike
With shiny, red, sparkling glitter on it,
It is brill.

Sharni-Jo Holloway (8)
Brookfield Primary School

THE DRAGON ROLLER COASTER

A Friday morning I went to the fair
And I rode the blue and red roller coaster
I rode the one up
        up
        up
        up
and drop
I gave a scream
It gave a scare
I felt my tummy go up
           up
           up
           up
           up
And I dare loop the loop
And I nearly felt sick
The roller coaster was high up
           up
           up
           up
I just look at the clouds and make pictures with them
And I see me open the scariest ride I have ever been on
the last loop the loop I went to the top of the hill
And drop
I gave a scream
It gave a scare
I felt my tummy go up
           up
           up
           up
           up
It had finished.

Molly Wright (8)
Brookfield Primary School

ANIMAL POEM

Rabbits thump
Kangaroos jump
Snakes glide
Birds hide
But I'm . . .
Sly.

Paul Brocklehurst (9)
Brookfield Primary School

THE CITY

Our city has big green trees
As big as a house
And we live in a house
It has bedrooms with a soft, comfy bed
And a giant toy box in the young children's room
In the mum's bedroom there is bright red lipstick.

Adam Cochrane (8)
Brookfield Primary School

THE EARTH

The Earth is round like a huge football
The Earth is green like a pencil green
I like the Earth because it's green and gigantic to see
The Earth is blue like a huge ocean.

Christien Davies (9)
Brookfield Primary School

EARLY MORNING

One early morning I flew to a place
And went somewhere called Florida
I saw Chip and Dale
Then I saw a baby whale.

One early morning I flew to a place
And went somewhere called Majorca
I met some friends called Kelly, Emma and Lauren
Then I asked if they were foreign.

One early morning I flew to a place
And went somewhere called London
I went to my friend, she was Lisa and met her at the museum
Then I went to see Liam.

One early morning I flew to a place
And went somewhere called Crete
I saw a mouse crawling and he said, 'Is your name Pete?'
Then I went to a restaurant then had some meat.

One early morning I flew to a place
And went somewhere called Kos
I saw a man crawling on the floor
Then he opened the bar door.

Abigail Reece (9)
Eastlands Junior School

BEACH

As I passed the beach
I saw the sea chewing up the shore
Towards the rock pools
And saw the sea silently snoring.

Adam Stuart Johnson (9)
Eastlands Junior School

MY AMAZING CAR JOURNEY

Car driving
As quick as a speedboat
Sister moaning
Like a tape recording every word she says
Dad groaning
As often as a bee buzzing
Noise deafening
Like a brick wall smashing
Suitcases crashing
As loud as a lion roaring
Cafés passing
Like big splodges of paint
Rain falling
As big as ancient mice
Map losing
Like a sweet raindrop gone forever.

Emma Jackson (9)
Eastlands Junior School

WHEN I WAS?

When I was one,
My life has just begun.
When I was two,
I learned to use the loo.

When I was three,
I learned to see.
When I was four,
I learned to open the door.

When I was five,
I learned to eat a pizza pie.
When I was six,
I learned to use matchsticks.

Jack Sadler (9)
Eastlands Junior School

MY AMAZING JOURNEY

One night I climbed into my book
And found I was in a posh racing car
I zoomed around the track and burnt up the tar
Then I destroyed my car.

One night I climbed into my book
And went swimming in the sea
I was hiding amongst the coral
Then jumped happily.

One night I climbed into my book
And landed in another world
I saw some strange and immoral people
The ugly sights unfurled.

One night I climbed into my book
And went swimming with an evil shark
I saw a massive alien
It landed on a park.

One night I climbed into my book
And saw Superman
He caught a robber in the bank
And foiled his evil plan.

Simon Leech (10)
Eastlands Junior School

A FANTASY JOURNEY

One night I climbed into a book
And I met Quentin Blake
And he taught me how to draw
Then he sketched me a beautiful cake

One night I climbed into a book
And went in the glass elevator
Then I went in the jungle with Tarzan
And wrestled an alligator.

One night I climbed into a book
And went to see J K Rowling
Then I played a Quidditch match
I love to be Harry Potter.

One night I climbed into a book
And went to meet the words
We met lots of authors
That was a night to remember.

David Jermy (10)
Eastlands Junior School

FIVE ANIMALS IN A JUNGLE

Down slithers the slimy snake
Scales all over its body
Lions leap for their prey again
Orange and yellow lion
That poor animal's pain

Monkeys swinging tree to tree
Naughty little liars
Lizards camouflaged in the colourful jungle
Catching flies as usual
Those flies should have known

Colourful parrot sitting on a tree
That colourful parrot keeps looking
At me until he falls out of the tree
With a *crash* and a *bang*
And a big *crack!*

Fiona Smith (8)
Eastlands Junior School

MY AMAZING JOURNEY

One exquisite day I climbed into a loft
And saw a lot of pictures
Of my grandad when he was two
And almost brand *new!*

One spectacular day I climbed into a loft
My nana was singing
She looked like Elvis
Shaking his pelvis!

One charming day I climbed into a loft
And zoomed into the 1960s
My mum looked like a stick insect
With a cat suit on
And men at her side.

One dull day I climbed into a loft
And went into space
I saw the sun
That looked like a hoop on fire.

One gloomy night I climbed into a loft
And saw myself, wow!
But I don't think you want to know.

Samantha Palmer   (9)
Eastlands Junior School

MY AMAZING BOOK JOURNEY

One day I climbed into a magical book
And found myself in a little cottage
I looked around for something to cook
Then I found old granny
She looked like a wrinkled up prune.

One day I climbed into a magical book
And found myself in another spooky world
I looked around for some creatures and saw a duck
Then I went and picked it up
It was as light as a feather.

One day I climbed into a magical book
And found myself in a dark, gloomy wood
I looked back and saw a hook
Then I looked again and saw it was Little Red Riding Hood
She had a cloak as red as a red rose

One day I climbed into a magical book
And found myself in a spotless, clean palace
I looked for my handsome prince and looked
Then I found my handsome prince
He was as gorgeous as gorgeous can be.

Chloe Greaves (10)
Eastlands Junior School

THE BEACH

As I pass the sandy beach
There's someone I'd like to meet
On the rocky roads I see
There's a head that's pleasant to see

As I pass the sandy beach
I see a face looking at me
Like a friend in the sea
Softly sleeping just like me.

Katie Hook (9)
Eastlands Junior School

ONE NIGHT I REACHED FOR THE STARS

One night I reached for the stars
But instead I got Mars
So I went into space
And got in a race
I won the race of course
And won the golden horse

I got into space
And put on the oxygen just in case
I landed in a gigantic bowl
And now I've got two pet moles
Now aren't I a lucky soul?

I put Mars back
And found a sack
You'll never guess what I found?
Three purple, snotty, spotty, shiny aliens not making a sound,
I took them out and put them on my bed
One climbed on my head
So now I've got . . .
Three smelly aliens
Two small moles
And one small, little planet called Mars
Now who's the lucky soul?

Sarah Hynes (10)
Eastlands Junior School

JOURNEY LEARNING

In the classroom
So small and warm
Don't be scared
    Not at all

In the classroom
So small and dark
Don't be scared
    Not at all

In the classroom
My journey carries on
I am not scared
    Not at all.

Beth Thompson (8)
Eastlands Junior School

UNTITLED

Cats are furry
Dogs are rough
Hares are fast
Fish are scaly
Snakes are slithery
Sheep are woolly
Horses are kickers
Pigs are smelly
And that's what
They are!

Beth Miles (8)
Eastlands Junior School

SPECIAL SPACE

Soon I was in space
And I was up to the test
The stars looked weird
The moon was the best.

Mars was red
Uranus was blue
The sun was orange
Like me and you.

Travelling from planet to planet
We were more tired every planet
Now we're off home
After our planet tour.

Ciaran Harvey (9)
Eastlands Junior School

A VIEW FROM HEAVEN

View from Heaven
Is such a beautiful sight
It's a lively looking land
Especially from this height

It's a whirling waiting world
From Heaven's view
I don't know the view down there
Do you?

I'm travelling to Heaven
Heaven is a peaceful place
It's full of old people
Everyone's got a wrinkly face.

Christopher Palmer (9)
Eastlands Junior School

IN THE JUNGLE

I was walking in the jungle
Something was moving in the tree
Could it be a lion
Looking for his tea?

I saw a big banana
Falling out a tree
Along came a monkey
And it shouted at me.

A snake slid past me
To go into the lake
A crocodile was sleeping
Then it was wide awake.

Josh Johnstone (8)
Eastlands Junior School

THE JOURNEY

Soon I was in space
You should have seen my face
It was a big disgrace
There was sick all over the place
I looked at the stars and Mars
It was a hard test
But Jupiter was the best.

There was Jupiter, Mars and Venus too
A creature popped out and said 'Boo!'
He gave me a clout
And I went *'Ouch!'*
That was my journey into space.

Sam Scott (9)
Eastlands Junior School

One Day I Climbed Into A Book

One day I climbed into a huge book
I saw some sparks so bright
With my head in dynamite
When my head came out
I heard a great, big shout

With a hole in the floor I wanted more
And I said let's visit another book

One day I climbed into a huge book
And, wow, a big house
Where I saw a little tiny mouse
It stood there without a care
It ran away when it saw me there.

Richard Cheshire (9)
Eastlands Junior School

My Journeys

I have journeyed far and wide
Since the day that I was born
I've been carried around corridors
And pushed down streets
I've slid down a slide
And fell in mud
I've walked to school and back
And I've felt very sad and very, very mad
I've been to Australia, San Marino and all
But my favourite journey of all is coming *home,*
Home is the bet place to be, if you're *me!*

Hollie Ashcroft (10)
Eastlands Junior School

A DAY IN LONDON

I went to London with the academy
Then found out that Adam was sitting on my knee.

I saw some scruffy tramps there
Then I found there was a spider in my hair.

Rachel fastened my clothes up for me
Then I found out that I was singing happily.

We walked across to the theatre
Then I found I had only walked a metre.

We went to McDonald's to get a Happy Meal
Then something fell off the bus it must have been the wheel.

Sophie Jerram (9)
Eastlands Junior School

HOW NEIL ARMSTRONG MET AN ALIEN

Neil climbed into his spaceship humming to himself
Excited about going into space
Jupiter was massive
While he was looking at spectrum
Something caught his eye
At first he thought it was Ryan C
But it was too ugly
Then he realised it was an alien
So he ran home screaming.

Amber Marie Burn (7)
Eastlands Junior School

ONE NIGHT I JUMPED INTO MY CAR

One night I jumped into my car
And drove along to Spain
I really thought there was going to be sun
But instead there was a lot of rain.

One night I jumped into my car
And drove far to the North Pole
I played ice hockey on the ice
Plus I scored a goal.

One night I jumped into my car
And drove all the way back home
My parents said 'We're going to Rome,'
But I went to bed instead.

Brad Drury (10)
Eastlands Junior School

FUTURAMA

One-eyed people walking around the streets
Spaceships flying in the air
Robots scaring old people
Never kissing the world goodbye

Time machines all over the city
Flying cars that won't get flat tyres
Aliens watching movies at the cinemas
Now it's the future
It will never end.

Joe Ives (8)
Eastlands Junior School

ONE NIGHT I WAS SUCKED INTO A GAME

One night I was sucked into a game
It was a ghostly graveyard
A man came out, he looked like my dad
They were exactly the same.

One night I was sucked into a game
I looked around
Then I heard a weird sound
It was like a spooky, black, midnight town.

One night I was sucked into a game
It was getting really, really creepy
I was beginning to feel really weary
It was like a freezing freezer.

Chantelle Lawson (9)
Eastlands Junior School

FUTURE

I'm in the future
It's cold and glittery
I'm in the future
From a time machine
I'm in the future
He, he, he, he, he
Kiss the future goodbye
Bye, bye, bye.

Ryan Childs (8)
Eastlands Junior School

MY JOURNEY

One night I went to London
And flew over the Queen
I took her crown which made her frown
And made the hundred year old woman scream

She told her guards (who couldn't run)
And chased me down the streets of town
With the Queen strolling behind
And she was still in her pink nightgown

Prince Charles jumped out the bakery shop
With his judo skills he couldn't be beaten
He got me down, like a magnet to the floor
And took the crown (million dollar)
And I was locked up in *jail.*

Jordan Jackson (10)
Eastlands Junior School

A POET HAS HIS OWN WORLD

When I sit down to write a poem
I enter my own world like a dream
I got to a mystical world with wizards
And unknown creatures
When I voyage through the worlds
I come to a stop at a blazing desert
Where the heat is intense
I shield my eyes from the sun
The light disappears
So I open my eyes
And there in front of me there are mermaids
Swimming around with King Neptune on his throne
But they were not the right poems.

Danny Sims-Waterhouse (8)
Eastlands Junior School

MYSTERIOUS ROCKY CELL

Tom will never tell
The story of the cell
The dangerous, spooky,
Pitch-black, gloomy
Creepy, scary cell
Tom will never tell.

Nathan Travis Shaw (7)
Eastlands Junior School

CRAB JOURNEY

Crabs look like lobsters finding its prey
Sucks up salt and seaweed, no time to play
Its journey will take them up to the rocks
Where fishermen often catch them in their lobster pots
Crabs never walk forward, only side to side
They can go slowly or fast jut like a fairground ride.

Jeavon Blake (8)
Eastlands Junior School

THE SEA

The waves waving
The sea's nice and calm
Fish leaping out of the sea
Sea shells shining
Motor boat going fast
Pupils sun bathing
Dogs playing
What a fab day!

Sean Palmer (7)
Eastlands Junior School

JOURNEYS

J ourneys are from
O ne place to another
U nderground, where it's dirty to
R ound a whizzing roundabout
N ext you might decide to go to
E ngland where it's always raining!
Y ou could go just anywhere
S o get packing now.

Vicky Bennett (8)
Eastlands Junior School

A MAGICAL PLACE

Up in the magical sky,
Where the angels fly high,
There's a magical, enchanted palace,
I wish I was there,
Up in the enchanted sky,
Where the angels fly high.

Christie Childs (8)
Eastlands Junior School

LONG AGO

Long, long ago
When the world was young
An egg was laid from a T-rex
Then he hatched and cracked
Waiting desperately for air . . .
Then it was gasping for air . . . dead!

Jordan Hallam (8)
Eastlands Junior School

SPRING

Spring is a story
Chapter one of life
The beginning of the beginning
Summer's wife.

Spring is a playground
Children having fun
Flowers bloom around them
And the morning sun.

Spring is a child
Learning and growing
Playful and energetic
Its joylessness showing.

Spring is a smile
A sign of joy
As summer comes
The children's toy!

Vanessa E Jenkins (11)
Peafield Lane Primary School

WHAT AM I?

Cabbage eater,
Winter sleeper.

Slow walker,
Sleepy stalker.

Claws sharper,
House harder.

Arron Lewis (10)
Peafield Lane Primary School

SPRING

Spring is an egg,
Newly hatched,
Showing its splendour.

Spring is a flower,
Blossoming beautifully,
Showing its colours.

Spring is a lamb,
Fresh as a daisy,
Brimming with life.

Spring is a story,
Read thousands of times,
But yet to be read.

Kate Filimon (10)
Peafield Lane Primary School

AUTUMN

Autumn is a fire
Blazing red, orange and yellow

Leaves are coloured jewels
Laying on a green velvet cloth

Leaves are cornflakes
Being crunched by boots

Corn is gold
Being taken from the fields

Autumn was a fire
Now it's a snowball across the globe.

Hannah Hammond (10)
Peafield Lane Primary School

WHAT AM I?

Bird - catcher
Wall - jumper
Fast - runner
Finger - snatcher
Nosy - sneaker
Heavy - sleeper
Cool - chiller
Chair - scratcher
Mouth - hisser
Ear - listener
Mouse - killer
Tummy - filler
Keen player

What am I?

Stephanie Kendall (10)
Peafield Lane Primary School

WHO AM I?

Big printer
Good for winter

Enormous walker
Non-human talker

Extinct eater
Huge seater

Put these together
I am a . . . mammoth.

Jessica Street (11)
Peafield Lane Primary School

WHO AM I?

Wet noser
Big barker

Fast licker
Small player

Little sleeper
Big eater

Good killer
Finger chewer

Who am I?
(My puppy Pippa)

Natalie Bouch (10)
Peafield Lane Primary School

AN EARTHQUAKE

Light flasher
Window smasher

Power cutter
Land nitter

Ground shaker
Noise maker

Long rumbler
Heavy bumbler.

Who am I?

Kieran Johnson (10)
Peafield Lane Primary School

WHO AM I?

A log picker
A water licker

A man rider
A long strider

A forest liver
Men quiver

Getting taller
A person caller.

Callam Green (10)
Peafield Lane Primary School

THE LADY FROM YORK

There was an old lady from York
Who swallowed a bad piece of pork
She went to bed
And hit her head
That was the old lady from York.

Hannah Wilkinson (11)
Peafield Lane Primary School

BUTTERFLIES

Butterflies flutter
Pretty colours, rainbow shades
Countryside colour.

Natalie Rowbottom (11)
Peafield Lane Primary School

SPACE RACE

Once there was a huge race in space
Which was brilliant, even ace
An alien crashed
An alien smashed
That's the huge race in space.

Aidan Reid (11)
Peafield Lane Primary School

THERE WAS A YOUNG LADY NAMED PERKINS

There was a young lady named Perkins,
Who loved to eat sour gherkins,
One day at tea,
She ate 43,
And pickled her internal workings.

Rebecca Ashford (10)
Peafield Lane Primary School

T-REX

T-rex
Hunting prey,
Eating them whole,
Menacing, fierce, horrible dinosaur,
Dangerous.

Thomas Price (10)
Peafield Lane Primary School

THE COOL SCHOOL

There was a fantastic new school,
The children were really cool,
They played on their scooters,
They pipped their hooters,
That's the fantastic cool school.

Gareth Wharmby (10)
Peafield Lane Primary School

CINQUAIN - LION CUB

Bloodthirsty creatures
Barbaric, brutal killers
Terrific scent to track down its prey
Lion cub.

Luke Parker (11)
Peafield Lane Primary School

MOUSE

Mouse
Soft fur
Hiding in a hole
Running away from eagle
Safe.

Stephen Malcolm (11)
Peafield Lane Primary School

BADGERS

Badgers
In the fresh grass
Playing in the warm den
Black and white, wet nose and sad eyes
Badgers.

James Cattanach (10)
Peafield Lane Primary School

TIGERS

Ripping flesh
Killing their prey
Striped bloodsucking beasts
Tigers.

Jay Theakstone (10)
Peafield Lane Primary School

TIGERS

Tigers
Agile and fast
Moving through the tall trees
Pouncing and biting its scared prey
Caught it.

Daniel Higgins (11)
Peafield Lane Primary School

MAN FROM MARS

There was an old man from Mars
Who ate a load of chocolate bars
He got up the next morning
To find himself bulging
That silly old man from Mars.

Jon Jack Miles (10)
Peafield Lane Primary School

RAPTOR

Raptor
Eating prey
Rippling its flesh
Ferocious, horrible, killing dinosaur
Warning!

Jake Hymas (11)
Peafield Lane Primary School

OWL

Nightmare animal
Cute, fluffy thing
Black pupils piercing eyes
Owl.

Sarah Jepson (10)
Peafield Lane Primary School

THE SILLY OLD LADY FROM FRANCE

There was an old lady from France
Who really loved to dance
She did the tango
And ate a mango
That silly old lady from France.

Natasha Garner (11)
Peafield Lane Primary School

SWIMMING

As I splish and I splash and I swim
On through the never ending sea
I splish and I splash from the man-eating sharks
Splish, splash, splish, splash, splish, splash.

Now I'm swimming through some murky water
My leg hits something hard
Suddenly a huge, monstrous crocodile pops
Out from the water
I swallow the water (disgusting.)

Now I'm in the sea near a fishing boat
They throw a net
It hits me
I sink
Down
And
Down
Next minute my mum calls me to come out . . .

Of the bath!

Sam Machin (9)
Ramsden Primary School

ME IN A DIFFERENT DIMENSION

I was playing in my garden
Suddenly
A beam came
And we shot up.

We appeared in a cave
The wall said
'Give me a machine
To let you go wherever you want
In this dimension.'

We went to a deep forest
With bats squealing
Snakes hissing
And dinosaurs.

We went to a village
With very small people
I found a black stone
And touched it
Time stopped
And I went home.

Nicholas Roberts (9)
Ramsden Primary School

MYSTERY

I'm green
I'm something beginning with 'L'
I'm Irish
I live in Ireland
Have you guessed it?
I'm a leprechaun.

When I go through a mirror
I go through a different dimension
I see the lost world below me
I come back into my bedroom
Take the costume off
It's after tea
Mum shouts

Homework!

Sophie Black (9)
Ramsden Primary School

THE ISLAND OF LAGOON

I go to my mum's room
I touch the mirror
It sucks me in
It hasn't done that before
Where will it take me?
It could lead me to an island
Or even a pit
. . . or the Island of Lagoon.

I was at an island
A small peasant owned it
He said 'Welcome to the Island of Lagoon'
. . . my Island of Lagoon.

There were so many mirrors
I couldn't get out
'Why don't you try that one?'
I did
I was back
. . . from the Island of Lagoon.

Edward Roberts (9)
Ramsden Primary School

HORSES

Let's go out
Trotting along paths,
Through the meadows and the silky grass.
Trotting through the rain,
Clip clop, clippety clop,
Along the winding paths,
Over the bumpy stones,
The saddle sliding.
Sweating as we ride,
Sweat dripping off the forelock.
Signs that we see when we quickly ride past.
Sweat and lather streaming off the horse's mane.
Over streams and even over hills and mountains.
The hooves start to slow
As we pass through the weaving grass,
But still rushing to get home.

So let's go home.

Rachel Darby (9)
Ramsden Primary School

SKIDDING

Tumbling down the snow-capped mountain
Crashing!
Whirling!
Snow splashes in the cold, wet face
I've got cold hands
Freezing bottom
The freezing cold bites
Cold, wet snow in my mouth
Skidding down in the freezing snow.

Alice Fenton (9)
Ramsden Primary School

CAR

My mummy in the car
On the stony road.
Up the road we went
On the bumpy stones.
We sing on the way
As the wheels go round.
Traffic lights we see
Shining very brightly.
Cars going fast
On the motorway.
Busy roads around
People on the pavement.
Skidding cars on roads
Travelling far away.

Grace Bowling (8)
Ramsden Primary School

FLYING CARPET

Sitting on my carpet
All brightly coloured
Just about to read
Whirl, turn, off in the sky
The birds pecked my nose
The magic carpet spoke
Stopped at the flying island to eat
Through clouds
Wind going through my hair
Landed in a skid
Went back to normal.

Rebecca Halpin (9)
Ramsden Primary School

SUB TRIP

I was going there and back,
The propeller whirling, whirling,
Looking through the steamed window
Watching, watching as the fish go by.
Fish of every colour and brightness,
I was going there and back.

I was going there and back,
And the monsters of the ocean
Lurking, lurking through the sea plants.
As we slept we heard a crash,
A ferocious shark in the distance
As we went there and back.

I was going there and back.
Shark of the ocean lashing, crashing,
Down to the bottom.
We were safe on the ocean.
We had been there and back.

Blake Moore (9)
Ramsden Primary School

HELICOPTER PILOT

I sit there listening to the spinning blades
Sitting there as the motors hum
Me, the fearless pilot
The blades trying to catch the other one in front
As we hover above the city
As we stop at airport cafes
As the blades turn, turn, turn.

Alexander Palfreyman (9)
Ramsden Primary School

VOYAGE

I was just looking at the mirror and
Suddenly
I'm on a flying island.
It smells like Mars bars.
A statue witch
And a flying carpet
Take me for a ride
Over the trees
Splashing the water
Whizzing through the air.
My hair blows back.
I see all the stars shining
    and I wake up.

Chad Gee (8)
Ramsden Primary School

A PERFECT DAY

We bob up and down
Fish shining in the sun.
Everyone was happy
In our big, glittery, gold dinghy.
The sun was shining down hard
People were swimming in the sea.
Ships were coming past, fast.
Children swimming with rubber rings.
The ice cream man was on the sand
People sunbathing on towels.
Big sandcastles by the sea.
Seagulls flying over us.
A perfect day.

Charlotte Bell (8)
Ramsden Primary School

FUTURE PLANET

I was only looking for something to drink,
When suddenly,
A control appeared in the cupboard!
The cupboard started to rattle.
My kitchen cupboard was a spaceship.
Suddenly it shot off.
I burst through the roof,
Leaving the kitchen table toasted.
I whizzed through the sky.
I crashed into another planet
Everything was strange.
There were flying cars,
Flying buildings,
Flying road signs
And people.
I realised
I was in the future!

Tim Bower (9)
Ramsden Primary School

THE KITCHEN MIRROR

Spider webs all over the mirror
Sitting on my carpet looking in
I drop the mirror
Smashing it across the floor
Wheels falling off the mirror
I took the mirror everywhere
Lovely patterns on a beautiful mirror
Glass mirror on the wall.

Natalie Plant (8)
Ramsden Primary School

Water-Skiing

Zooming across the ocean
Water splashing behind me
Feeling the wind going through my hair
It made me hungry
Smashing through the waves
Leaping from the boat
Hanging on a piece of string
Struggling to stand up on my skis
I leapt into the air
I looked behind me
There was a ramp
I landed with a
Crash!

Vincent Rodgers (9)
Ramsden Primary School

The Flying Island

I was just looking into the mirror
Then suddenly
I was on a big flying island
With friendly people walking by
Local shops and newsagents opening
The noise of horns and bells
Church bells ringing
Footsteps on the path
I stay for a while
Then step back home.

Joshua Wright (8)
Ramsden Primary School

A SPECIAL DELIVERY

In a letter box down the street,
I picked up a letter and both my feet
Got sucked into the letter box,
Don't know why,
And for some reason go travelling by.

Through time go back straight like a dream,
And all of a sudden begin to seem
Like I'm decades younger
Than I was last year,
And I met Queen Victoria
Standing near.

Dark skirts gleaming round women's legs,
Horses' hooves on cobbled streets.
Women look posh with covered ankles,
Men walk by and look quite neat.
Burnt black sky with hurricane clouds,
Choirs singing very loud
With brass bands playing in the park,
Time to go home, it's getting dark.

Now where is that letter box?

Adam Brunyee (8)
Ramsden Primary School

UNDER AND OVER THE SEA

Red submarines bashes,
Swim for your life!
Yellow cruise ship crashes,
Swim for your life!

Life boats come to rescue us,
For this the end of our cruise,
Dinghies empty and full.

Sharks chase you in the water
Snapping at you fiercely.
He's just about to catch me!
Oh no! He's broke my flipper.

Deeper, deeper, deeper
They dive, searching
Amongst the rubble.

Relieved people ride on
Brave dolphins to shore.

Survivors stand
In the harbour, shivering,
Children weep at the loss of parents.

Richard Tricklebank (8)
Ramsden Primary School

ME, MY DAD AND A MOTORBIKE

My dad was down the straight,
He saw a great big crate,
He went past me and his cool mate,
And I thought he was really great,
My mum came through the gate,
With me, my dad and a motorbike.

My dad's motorbike couldn't stay cool,
My mum went playing pool,
I went and sat on a stool,
Then I felt like a mule,
I'd lost my favourite tool,
With me, my dad and a motorbike.

I was having a lot of fun,
Then I went and lifted a ton,
My nana came with mum,
And made me a great big bun,
And suddenly my dad had won,
With me, my dad and a motorbike.

Jack Lilliman (10)
Robert Jones Junior School

THE MONSTER AND HIS CAR

The monster went to the bar
In his flashy new car
He doesn't live that far
He lives with a guitar
The monster and his car
The car likes mice
They're very nice
In a chunky slice
At a good bar.

The monster's name is Jack
He won't come back
He's got a big back
When he's got a pack
At a good bar
The car likes chicks
When their name is Mick
That's a tasty pick
The monster and his car.

James Dopson (11)
Robert Jones Junior School

FISH FACE

Dad ate a fish
And gave out a wish
And it landed on my dinner dish
I said to the plate
Go on let's be mates
Oh I don't have to wait

We went to the pool
It swam to keep cool
Then we had a game of pool
He liked to moan
So we had to go home
Plates have mates
But they have to wait

To finish off
We went to the shop
And he hopped.

Whitney McAllister (9)
Robert Jones Junior School

Outside My Bedroom Window

I woke up this morning
And everyone was yawning
And on the TV
That includes me!
I looked at the sea
Outside my bedroom window
And then I made sure
The sea was ashore
Then guess what I saw
And I wanted more
Then I saw some sweets
Walking down the streets
Outside my bedroom window
Then I saw a man
Standing on a van
Then on the street
Guess who to meet
Outside the bedroom window.

Cassy Chandler (10)
Robert Jones Junior School

Growing Up

We have all moved to different places
Ready for other people to go in our spaces
I remember my dolls and toys
Now I'm into handsome boys
We all have to go through the thing that we hate
Yes, we have to go through the school gate.

All of the stupid white lies I've told
They have all worn away now I'm getting old
But even if it does come to an end
There's one thing I'll never lose my friends
Yes I'll get married, yes I'll have a family
But there's nothing that will change my friends and me.

Elizabeth Topliss (11)
Robert Jones Junior School

HAIKUS

The Fuzzy Prickly Monster

I saw a monster
A big, fuzzy, prickly one
Then it ate me up

The Haunted House

It is haunted lots
And it is very scary
The old haunted house

Under the Sea

You will like it lots
Visit me under the sea
It is very fun

The Merry-Go-Round

The merry-go-round
Goes round and round all day long
Then she falls to sleep.

Ashlene Bagshaw (11)
Robert Jones Junior School

THE BOY CALLED JIM

There was a boy called Jim
And he couldn't even swim
He had a friend called Sam
Who loved to eat jam
His mum was called Jill
And his dad was called Bill
His brother was called Phil
And his sister was called Lil
So that made him the odd one out
So he had to always shout.

Jim says 'Why am I odd?'
His mum says 'Because you're a little sod!'
One day his mum shouted 'Jim!'
Come downstairs you need a trim
His mum said 'Your hair is frizzy
So we better get busy!'

Mellissa Donkin (11)
Robert Jones Junior School

FWSS

Blazing flames glowing,
Sizzling, scorching, burning fire,
Red, orange, yellow.

Soggy, damp and wet,
Drenched, water, showers of rain,
Cold, flowing water.

Red-hot, sizzling sun,
Boiling, bright, sunny sunshine,
Bubbling, hot flames.

Freezing cold, wet white,
Frosty snowballs and snowmen,
Cold, bright, deep white snow.

Francesca Eaton (11)
Robert Jones Junior School

OUR TEACHER

There was a teacher from Spain,
Who had an enormous brain,
She teaches maths
And learns at the swimming baths.
She moans all day,
And we can't get away,
As she just shouts straight away.
'Miss I need the loo' you would shout,
And then you must get out straight away,
Then that's it, she's in a mood,
Because this boy won't stop being rude,
And she screamed away.

That's when we cover our ears,
Because she's as loud as six fields being cut down,
She collects our books,
Then this boy shouts 'This is boring,'
So she shouts 'Just ignore him,'
And next day miss is away,
    That's our teacher!
    We all shout *'That's our teacher!'*

Siobhan Allen (11)
Robert Jones Junior School

THE INVISIBLE MAN!

Once I was walking down the street,
Then who do you think I should meet?
Someone who had funny feet,
Walking wobbly down the street,
Walking down the street.

I think he followed me home,
I heard him starting to moan,
And suddenly he's gone,
I think a light just shone,
Oh no, no.

Looking round the garden,
Looking in the house,
Running around the streets,
And looking with the mouse.

Charlotte Youngs (9)
Robert Jones Junior School

THE WONDERFUL BAND

There was a wonderful band,
Who played mostly on the sand,
And were famous all over the land.

They played so very fast,
That they never came last,
Everyone else they pass.

C'mon now's the time
To get in line,
To follow the big entry sign.

Gemma Harris (10)
Robert Jones Junior School

HENRY THE ALIEN

I know a Henry,
Henry is an alien,
He's very podgy.

He's covered in slime,
On his gross feet are huge hats,
He's like a round bowl.
He's a giant ball,
He's got ears like a mouse,
His planet is Zurg.

Ninety-two Warloo,
Warloo is his street, *weirdo!*
Aliens are weird.

Eve Wilkins (9)
Robert Jones Junior School

THE ICE BOY

There was a cool ice man,
He was called Icy Ice,
He rode in an ice cream van,
And he's a chilly ice man.

He's like an icicle,
Sometimes he rides a bicycle,
He's fresh and frosty,
And he's the ice man.

All he eats is ice cream,
And all he drinks is water,
And he's the cool Icy Ice.
The Ice Boy.

Janece Gaskell (11)
Robert Jones Junior School

MY MUM THE BABOON

My mum the baboon,
She always was a goon,
She ran around the room,
And stared at the white moon,
My mum the baboon.
My mum the baboon,
She looked like a big balloon,
She was certainly sure to pop soon,
My mum the baboon.
My mum the baboon,
She eats with a shiny silver spoon,
My mum the baboon.

My mum the baboon,
She made a big yellow cocoon,
And had a black and yellow harpoon,
But then it exploded, boom!
My mum the baboon.
My mum the baboon,
She likes sweeping with the broom,
It was a very sunny afternoon,
My mum the baboon.
My mum the baboon,
Her favourite cartoon is the Loony Toon,
Her favourite food is a big mushroom,
My mum the baboon!

Samson Pratley (10)
Robert Jones Junior School

THE CREATURE

It was a deadly night,
For the boat on the splashing waves,
The sea was like a pouncing tiger,
Gobbling up everything including caves.

Then all of a sudden,
What a frightful thing,
There it was,
With its fin,
A creature from the deep blue sea.

With its evil eyes,
Staring back up at me,
It tried to attack with its jagged teeth,
But fortunately it missed,
That creature under the colourful reef.

Rebecca Bailey (10)
Robert Jones Junior School

DALMATIAN PLANTATION

Shall we have a Dalmatian Plantation?
It will surely be an inspiration.
We will invite all the nation,
It will be a sensation.
The biggest Dalmatian was called Snot,
People say he was a Dalmatian, surely not?
Because instead of having a big, round spot,
They were as small as a dot.
The smallest was called Lucky,
Who likes to get really mucky.

Liam Pride (10)
Robert Jones Junior School

THE ICE TEACHER

A nice ice teacher
A teacher made of gold ice
Ever so unkind.

She's a big werewolf
Interested in skating
She's like a thick-o.

She's got a huge flag
She never knows what to do
She's not got a brain.

She likes Craig David
She dislikes all bad language
She's very horrid.

Amanda Holmes (10)
Robert Jones Junior School

THE WIZARD OF WASHINGTON

There was a wizard of Washington,
He slipped on a welly and felt his fat belly,
He decided to zap himself and be renamed to Nelly.

One fine day he decided to play leap frog with his huge belly,
He cried aloud 'Help me, I'm round and I'm flat on the ground
And I need to go and play with Kelly' (his dog!)

On the very next day his witchcraft and wizardry fines,
And that's Nelly the wizard of Washington
Doing what does almost every day (badge up.)

Paul Tongue (10)
Robert Jones Junior School

THE FLESH EATING FLEA

One day you'll see the flesh eating flea
It goes everywhere, but it came to me
It's a creepy, crawling, climbing beast
It'll appear right there once you're having a feast

It happened to me so why not to you?
It will hide in your clothes or even your shoe
It's a tiny, teeny, travelling thing
It will appear in your jewellery, necklace or ring

I don't know how it could get here
But now it's here that is clear
I don't know why it came to me
And that's the poem of the flesh eating flea.

Fiona Booth (10)
Robert Jones Junior School

THE SPIDER

I am terrified
I am scared
The spider moves quickly and creepily
The spider's body is round, fat and long
Hairy legs go tap, tap, tap
Googly eyes looking at me
It came down the wall on to me
'Help!' I cried
My mum came in with a newspaper
Splat! It's dead
Splattered on the wall
My mum puts him in tissue
And flushes it down the loo!

Jessica Caudwell (10)
St John's CE Primary School, Worksop

ARACHNAPHOBIA

It makes me feel nervous
A wreck even
Its venomous fangs dripping with venom
It moves towards me sneakily, slyly, stalkingly, creepily
It plays havoc with my nerves, I'm arachnaphobic
Now it's on my leg in full detail
Its red, pulsating, spiny abdomen
With a green, slimy thorax
Its bloodthirsty fangs about to bury into my delicate skin
I shall be poisoned if I shout my mum, for it will get scared and so
                                                            will I

Suddenly the lights flicker out
I'm alone in the dark
A wave of terror strikes me
I can't breathe
Suddenly I jerk upright in bed with cold sweat dripping
The nightmare is over.

Adam Betts (10)
St John's CE Primary School, Worksop

SPIDER

I feel scared and freaked out
I feel like screaming
I daren't move
It's moving slowly and sneakily, creepily
Its body is round, its eyes are goggily
It has eight long, hairy legs
It's huge
I know the spider is more scared than I am
Because I'm bigger than he is
But I'm still scared.

Bianca Holland (10)
St John's CE Primary School, Worksop

THE SPIDER

I'm nervous
I'm scared
I want my mum to help me
But she's not there!
My mum has left me for the night
And spiders give me the most terrible fright
They gave me a fright at the very first sight
But the good thing is that they only come out at night
It's nearly at the top of my bed
I hope it doesn't climb on my head
My mum suddenly comes in and splatters it flat
And all my mum says is 'That is that!'

Leah Abbs (9)
St John's CE Primary School, Worksop

THE SPIDER

Spiders are big, spiders are small,
Spiders are creepy, they make your blood freeze,
They're hairy, they're scary,
Money spiders to tarantulas,
Some are small and friendly,
Some are hairy and scary,
They can hang on the ceiling,
Hang on the wall,
Some are as big as a ball,
Some with green eyes,
Some with blue,
Look out! It's coming after you.

Jamie Bonser (10)
St John's CE Primary School, Worksop

THE CHAIR

I wake up in the morning
Just as the day is dawning
I go down the stairs and sit at the table
On the table is a parcel with a red label
I open all the layers
I give it a few tears
I open the parcel, let's see what's in it
There's a chair in the parcel where you can sit
'Wow, look at this!' I say
'This is the right thing to sit in the garden in May'
I put the chair in the hall
I put it next to a wall which is tall
I slip the chair to my room
I keep looking at it while I watch my cartoon
I was so happy with my chair
So I left the chair there.

Kirsty Hayes (8)
St John's CE Primary School, Worksop

SPIDER ATTACK

Scared, frightened as they move towards me I feel I need to scream
But they're coming one by one working as a team
Its venomous fangs showing, its long teeth even
They're just above her, 10cm away
Nervous as a wreck, cunningly, stiffly it moves
But I will start hating spiders now
It starts to move down the wall getting closer
It drops on to the bed, she moves towards the door
It moves too, I slammed the door and ran down the stairs to my mum.

Robyn Lloyd (10)
St John's CE Primary School, Worksop

THE LOST CITY

The lost city
Spooky and dark
And lonely
It goes every night
The spooks comes out
To see the lights
Rise in the air
The ghosts say
'Aaaaaaah.'

The lost city
Spooky and dark
And lonely
It goes every night
The spooks come out
To see the light
Rise in the air
The zombies say
'Aaaaaaah.'

Daniel Edwards (8)
St John's CE Primary School, Worksop

SPACE

Space, space is a wonderful place,
When you go up there it'll be a big place,
You'll go past Mercury, Pluto and the moon,
Space, space is a wonderful place.

Tom Pieroni (9)
St John's CE Primary School, Worksop

A NONSENSE POEM

Girls are girls,
Boys are boys,
Girls like twirls,
Boys like toys.

Cats are cats,
Dogs are dogs,
Cats like mats,
Dogs like frogs.

Tigers are tigers,
Lions are lions,
Tigers like fingers,
Lions like dandelions.

Girls and boys,
Cats and dogs,
Tigers and lions,
What no frogs!

Stephen Latham (7)
St John's CE Primary School, Worksop

FAIRIES

I dream about fairies
Christmas tree fairies
Daisy fairies
Every fairy has different coloured wings
Every fairy loves to sing
Under the mushroom the fairies live
Playing together happily.

Caroline Hardy (7)
St John's CE Primary School, Worksop

I LIKE EVERYTHING

Hot countries,
Cold countries,
Every country,
A nice country,
Big or small,
I like everything.

Hot weather,
Cold weather,
Every weather's good weather,
Rain or shine,
I like everything.

Hot food,
Cold food,
Every food's a good food,
Spicy or sweet.
I like *everything*.

Chloe Slater (8)
St John's CE Primary School, Worksop

DRAGONS

Dragons are big
Dragons are scary
Dragons are fierce
You should be wary

Dragons are huge
They even eat tyres
They live in caves
They even make fires.

Matthew Roys (8)
St John's CE Primary School, Worksop

FOOTBALL

F   ootball is brill and exciting
O   h Booth has won the cup
O   zzie the Owl is on the pitch
T   en goals for Wednesday
B   eckham is crying
A   rsenal is winning a game for once
L   eeds losing the cup
L   eicester is defeated and the whistle has gone

Michael Hale (11)
St John's CE Primary School, Worksop

RAIN, RAIN IS A PAIN

Rain, rain is a pain
It goes down the lane
Rain, rain is a pain
It sees Jane
Rain, rain is a pain
It goes down the drain to Spain.

Francesca Withers (9)
St John's CE Primary School, Worksop

COLD

Snow is slushy and mushy
Snow is thick and thin
Snow is cold
Snow is old
Snow is white and cold.

Lewis Caudwell (8)
St John's CE Primary School, Worksop

BALLS

Balls are good
Balls are big
Balls you can kick
Balls can bounce
Balls are hard
Balls are good to play with
Balls can roll
Balls you can head.

Jordan Anthony Webster (11)
St John's CE Primary School, Worksop

SPLISH, SPLASH THERE GOES THE RAIN

Rain, rain, splish, splish
Rain, rain, it's very wet
Rain, rain, it's good for my plants
Rain, rain, it's down the lane
Rain, rain, you're a pain.

Bethany Ashmore (9)
St John's CE Primary School, Worksop

UP IN THE SKY

Up in the sky
Way up in the sky
And a star so high
The star so bright and light
Shine so high in the sky.

Wendy Mullen (8)
St John's CE Primary School, Worksop

SPACE

Space, space is a wonderful place
Say the people that have been there
Twinkling stars all over the place
Astronauts say they found a lace
Whoever goes always stays
Space, space, space.

Daniel Lilley (8)
St John's CE Primary School, Worksop

SPACE IS THE PLACE

Space, space
When you're in a spaceship you float around
120 planets as you turn around
The more planets you see
The more excitement it will be.

Matthew Coulton (8)
St John's CE Primary School, Worksop

I HATE RAIN

I hate rain
And it's a pain
Here it comes again
My sisters think it's good
As good as Yorkshire pud.

Alex Radford (8)
St John's CE Primary School, Worksop

SPACE, THE WONDERFUL PLACE

Space, space is a wonderful place
A wonderful place is space
It glows in the dark, it has no sharks
Space, the wonderful place
Space is my kind of place
I get there in a rocket
It takes me to the place
Space, space, the wonderful place.

Kieran Morris Owen (9)
St John's CE Primary School, Worksop

RAIN THE PAIN

Rain, rain, a bit of a pain
But it's not as if it will cane
It will come down from the sky
Like a big cherry pie
And get ready
It might hit you in the eye.

Thomas Jeffery (9)
St John's CE Primary School, Worksop

IN SPACE

Space is a place,
Where you walk at a slow pace,
Jupiter, Mars, stars, jars and
That's what you see in space.

Heather Allanson (9)
St John's CE Primary School, Worksop

Rain Is A Pain

I was in Spain, it was a pain
Because all it did was rain
I looked out my window
I saw the rain hitting the window
Rain, rain, such a pain
Just like my sister Jane.

Kristy Wright (9)
St John's CE Primary School, Worksop

Space

Space, space is the best ever place
Whoever goes up goes all over the place
They go up in a rocket
They come down in a pod
They land in the sea
I wish it was me.

Ben Day (8)
St John's CE Primary School, Worksop

Space

I went to space
I found a lace
So I went to the place
To find a case
The case was the place to space
I like the space to stay.

Julianne Simmen (9)
St John's CE Primary School, Worksop

THE SPIDER

I feel quite scared
And the eight evil eyes are looking at me
It is moving slowly towards me
With an evil look on its face
Its body is long and black
It has sharp fangs, red legs and spikes on its back
It's moving towards me ready to bite
I was frightened
Splat! I'm not frightened anymore
My mum killed it.

Marc Preston (10)
St John's CE Primary School, Worksop

RAIN

The rain is a pain,
It gets you all wet,
As if you're in a net,
The rain has power,
Like a flower.

Naomi Widdowson (8)
St John's CE Primary School, Worksop

ONE DAY MY HOUSE WAS CRAZY

My mum was on the stairs
She jumped off, there were bears!
She used to be lazy
Now she says 'I will not be lazy again.'

Scott McGough (7)
St John's CE Primary School, Worksop

THE SPIDER

The spider made me scared,
I daren't move an inch.
The spider just kept moving,
I was terrified.
As it came closer,
I saw most of its body,
Its big, large, gloomy eyes,
Its big, hairy legs moving one by one.
The spider's legs looked dry,
It then crept and looked all around,
It looked at me,
    I left the room . . .

Hannah Thompson (10)
St John's CE Primary School, Worksop

SPIDER

I feel scared, freaked out and panicky
It is moving quickly to me
Big and round like a ball
His legs are long and hairy
The spider is black with eight eyes and eight legs
He has green knobbly knees
His eyes are all focused on me because I can feel it
He is getting closer and closer by the minute
He dropped down and fell on me
His steamy breath hitting my face
His fangs snapping
I ran out of the room!

Lucy Shaw (9)
St John's CE Primary School, Worksop

NONSENSE POEM

I like beans
I like carrots
I like peas
I like maggots

I like rain
I like snow
I like Teletubbies
My best is Po

I like animals
I like dogs
I like beavers
Eating logs.

Jacob Fogg (8)
St John's CE Primary School, Worksop

THE SPIDER

If I saw a spider I would feel spooked,
Frightened and scared
But the spider I saw moved slyly,
Slowly and cunningly.
The spider had long legs, a red body and red eyes,
The spider's legs are delicate and hairy,
He looks like he is about to pounce at me and spit poison,
Those red eyes of evilness stare,
It came closer and closer to me,
I scream really loud and wake up.

Richard Delaney (9)
St John's CE Primary School, Worksop

THE MOUNTAIN OF WONDER

As the children walked in
The lights shone upon them
The scent of candy
Met their noses
The mountain shut
For evermore.

They listened to the sweet, soothing music
As they ate their delicious feast
They had forgotten about parents
But their parents had not forgotten them
The children began singing and playing
For evermore.

The mountain had marvellous candy walls
A swimming pool of glistening blue
And a golden beach
The mountain had countless
Rooms full of sweets
The children were in paradise
And they would be for evermore.

Laura Cunnington (9)
St John's CE Primary School, Worksop

THE SPIDER

There's a giant spider in my room
With eight fat legs and a nose like a broom
It turns to me, it just can't be
You won't believe it, it stares at me
I couldn't stand that evil eye
So I screamed and it made me cry.

Lauren Birch (9)
St John's CE Primary School, Worksop

THE PLANETS

We all live on planet Earth
This is where we had our birth
Our neighbour is the dusty moon
I would like to go there soon.

Jupiter has a giant spot
Venus is extremely hot
Pluto is furthest away
Rockets need to be faster than today.

These are planets in the sky
I will watch them as time goes by.

Conor Pollard (7)
St John's CE Primary School, Worksop

THE SPIDER

The spider was moving
I was shivering
Its fangs were dripping
Its nearly dribbling
I was terrified
Could I run?
No, my body froze
It's hanging on the ceiling
Right over my head
Well what a surprise
It's just tickled my head.

Stephanie Spence (10)
St John's CE Primary School, Worksop

THE BUNGEE JUMP

I'm scared
No you're not
Yes I am!

I'm not going to do it
Yes you are
No I'm not.

I've changed my mind, I'm going to do it
OK then do it
No I'm not going to do it
I'll push you then . . .
Aaah, I did it.

Thomas Moore (8)
St John's CE Primary School, Worksop

THE SPIDER

The spider crept towards me,
I felt nervous.
All I could do was watch,
Nothing could distract me from this vicious creature.
Blazing red eyes and thorax the size of a football
And fangs sharp and pointed.
It was climbing up my arm,
I started to sweat then *whack!*
The spider was dead.

Christian Ashton (10)
St John's CE Primary School, Worksop

THE MARVELLOUS MOUNTAIN

The children are led
By a mysterious man

Into a marvellous mountain
Into a mountain that's different
Into a mountain with animals
Into a mountain with games
Into a mountain with chocolate rivers
Into a mountain with flowers of every kind
Into a mountain with music
Into a mountain with beautiful lights
Into a mountain without any parents

They say they want to go higher
Higher into a cave

Into a cave with chocolate bats
Into a cave with friendship
Into a cave that is rich and beautiful

Soon after a day or two
Parents are forgotten
And they live for ever and ever.

Christopher Blood (9)
St John's CE Primary School, Worksop

DIFFERENT KINDS OF PEOPLE

People are big and small
People are short and tall
And do different things too
People dance and play every day
And in a different kind of way.

Abbie Gray (7)
St John's CE Primary School, Worksop

THE MOUNTAIN HOUSE

A strange man walked up the hill,
As large as a tiger,
The mountain opened as the children went in,
The music went on like a flowing river,
When the children went in they had a great feast,
After that they played games and sang songs,
At night they read books,
Forever long.

They woke up to games and breakfast,
After that they went to the beach,
The waves overlapped like hairs on a teddy bear,
And went to a cave of friendship.
They played together and sang together
Which made them very happy,
Forever friends.

Sarah Beardsley (9)
St John's CE Primary School, Worksop

THE SPIDER

I didn't like it as the spider moved towards me
It didn't seem slow or it didn't seem fast
Its body was gigantic with big, hairy legs
The spider looked at me with its big, beady eyes.

I watched every step and every move
As the spider came towards me
I thought in my head 'Please don't hurt me, just take my ted'
Suddenly as it was nearly here
I woke up from my worst fear.

Aaron Magor (10)
St John's CE Primary School, Worksop

KOPPELBERG HILL

As the children followed the music man,
The hill opened its lips,
The children overbalanced and fell in,
The marvellous, magical music man,
Led the children onwards,
To the underground seaside.

Every child was playing,
The marvellous magical music man
Played music for them,
The children made friends,
The music man played with them.

The children were devastated,
When they had to sleep,
But their beds were soothingly soft,
And the marvellous, magical music man
Played sweet, soft music for them.

Hannah Latham (9)
St John's CE Primary School, Worksop

THE MAGIC MOUNTAIN

The children peered at the mysterious mountain,
As the ground began to quiver,
The gigantic mountain opened its mouth,
And swallowed the children,
All the food was fit for a king,
All laid out on a long, wide table,
The children listened to the music,
Forgetting all about their crying parents.

Amy Chadwick (9)
St John's CE Primary School, Worksop

THE WONDERFUL CAVE OF DREAMS

The children gazed up at the magical mountain,
when they heard the sweet soft sound of
the piper's flute,
The children started skipping and running
up to the magical place.
It opened its beautiful wide entrance.

A new world here of beaches and waterfalls
with tango and chocolate coming down,
Colourful animals with bright coats
A soft slow river meandering
through the sand,
Palm trees made of chocolate and candy.

Through the sound of the beautiful waterfall,
the children could hear the entrance closing,
Closed forever,
Never to be opened.

Ben Dixon (9)
St John's CE Primary School, Worksop

ANNABEL

Annabel my baby is so cute
I love to put her in her little bed
She sleeps so soundly in her bed
When she wakes she makes *such a row!*
But I love her very much.

Anna Follows (7)
St John's CE Primary School, Worksop

NUMBER POEM

Fun
Moo
I need the loo
Me
Hall
I need more
Hi
Pie
I want to die
Devon
Mate
You want a fight?
Mine
Len
I climbed in the den
Clever
Weather
I caught a feather.

Chloe Pettinger (10)
St John's CE Primary School, Worksop

THE MOUNTAIN

The music went into the mountain hall
And the children followed
All around were stalactites
Pointing like fingers
Waterfalls shone as bright as diamonds
Tigers and lions were softer and gentler
They rode on their backs
And forgot about home.

Jason Lowe
St John's CE Primary School, Worksop

THE MYSTERIOUS MOUNTAIN

As the children approached
The magical, mysterious mountain,
The luxury inside could be seen,
The children clattered and clattered,
They jumped in,
The mountain closed with a bang,
It was sensational and amazing,
To wake up to music and games,
The music of the piper was mystical,
It flowed on and on,
Never stopping.

Simon Branch (10)
St John's CE Primary School, Worksop

THE DINOSAUR THAT FELL

I saw a dinosaur
He was sat on a wall
As I walked past he started to fall
He fell and fell and hit the ground
An ambulance came with a ne-nor sound
They put him on a stretcher
And carried him to the van
I think he's broken his leg
Said the ambulance man
His leg was in plaster for a month and a day
Oh how he wished he could go out and play.

Laura Smith (10)
St John's CE Primary School, Worksop

MY FAMILY

My family:

Mum is a washing machine
that spins around.
My mum is the warmth
in the house.

My family:

Dad is the winning goal,
Dad's the wind and rain.

My family:

Sister is a muddy face
Dirty clothes
It's war.

My family:
That leaves me
It's a long story

Jodie Rebekah Camm (10)
St John's CE Primary School, Worksop

RICKY'S FIRST GOAL

James Wood catches it
Passes it to James Hurt
Down the line to Mitchell Bead
Then through the middle to Ricky Machin
Who shoots
It's in, it's wide?
Goal!

Ricky Machin (10)
St John's CE Primary School, Worksop

OH MUM!

My mum says
When I was your age
I wasn't cheeky to my mum,
I always did what she said,
Oh mum!
Blah, blah, blah, blah, blah
Shut up!

My dad says
When I was your age
We played outside all day long
Throwing eggs at windows
Throwing ourselves on the road,
Hopscotch on the pavement.

That's not all, it gets worse!

Leanna Elizabeth Wilson (10)
St John's CE Primary School, Worksop

GHOSTS

Ghosts are white
Ghosts are bright
Ghosts are pains
That rattle chains
Some that groan
Some that moan
Some give you a fright
And some that are polite
They are mean
And can't be seen.

Hollie Munn (7)
St John's CE Primary School, Worksop

MY DOG

I miss his wagging little tail,
I miss his howling and his wail.
I miss his happy, loving glance,
I miss his circling, welcome dance.

I miss his little brown paws,
I miss his fighting dog wars.
I miss his big, rolling ball,
I miss his squealing, howling call.

Big ones, small ones,
Thin or fat!
I'd rather have one than a cat!

Katie Hanson (7)
St John's CE Primary School, Worksop

BEYOND THE LIMIT

Deep, deep in the cold, wet, freezing winter of the arctic snow
Suddenly from a mountain top
An avalanche begins to fall
Like an earthquake coming right at you
At 100 miles an hour
Risking a dangerous death
I run to a safe place to get away
The snow was getting closer and closer
The animals were running and just then
It stopped the way it was
The animals went back to the sea and I went on and on.

Richard Boyfield (10)
St John's CE Primary School, Worksop

A FOOTBALL GAME

One, nil
The goalie feels ill
One, all
The striker feels tall.
Two, one
The defence is gone.
Two, all
The coach makes a call,
Three, two
The subs are new,
Three, all
The whistle blows.
How much relief?
Nobody knows.

James Wood (11)
St John's CE Primary School, Worksop

DRAGON MCFLEE

There was a monster called McFlee,
Who never missed eating a bee.
He came from Zog
And lived in a log
In 1993!

There was a monster called McFlee,
Who never missed eating a bee.
He had the fleas
And liked swinging in trees
In 1993.

Samantha Mawson (8)
St John's CE Primary School, Worksop

THE ARCTIC

I am walking through the frigid Iceland
Polar bears roaring, penguins quacking
Snowflakes dropping on my head
Wind's so hard it's blowing the polar bears' fur
Frantically about
Ice in the sea
Sailing out into the Pacific
Overcast in the sky
Penguins duelling over fish
Walruses moaning ahead on the ice pieces
Killer whales jump in the icy water
In this frigid Iceland.

Scott Noble (10)
St John's CE Primary School, Worksop

THE JUNGLE

I am walking through the jungle,
A hot sweat comes across my face,
I feel tired as I get deeper,
Deeper into the jungle.

An enormous, slimy, scaly snake slithers past me,
My heart pounds,
Like a huge steam engine.

I feel so sleepy,
I must rest,
Beneath a tree I close my eyes,
And dream of home.

Rebecca Martindale (10)
St John's CE Primary School, Worksop

THE GREAT MOUNTAIN

As the children walked up
Their minds were on the mountain
The great mountain face opened its mouth
And in went the children
The mountain face shut
Forever shut.

The inside full of food
The children had such fun
They ate, sang and danced
They played games and fell asleep
Forever fun.

They felt so good
The fun was still there
They forgot all their homes
And forgot their parents
And every child was brother and sister.

Steven Woodcock (10)
St John's CE Primary School, Worksop

DAVID

D   is for dog which I have in my house
A   is for apple, red and shiny
V   is for vegetable that helps you grow
I   is for ink which we use to write
D   is for David which is my name.

David Hanson (8)
St John's CE Primary School, Worksop

THE COLD WORLD

I am walking through a cold world
An icy cold world.
As I am walking I can hear the wind howling
And the snow crunching under my feet.
I am walking through the snow,
Feeling cold I am walking into the mist and I see . . .
Five fluffy seals.
I am walking cat-like,
The wind blows the snowfoxes' fur
And they run away.
I am left on my own
So I walk away from the cold world.

Charlotte Field (9)
St John's CE Primary School, Worksop

ARCTIC

I don't know where I am?
It's cold and white
Like paper
I can hear the wind
It's as cold as a refrigerator
The cold concussing creepy snow
It hits you sharp . . . like a knife
I can see the wasteland
I don't know where I am
But I want to go home.

Jonathan Stretton (10)
St John's CE Primary School, Worksop

THE DREAM MOUNTAIN

They flowed in softly and slowly
The floor sparkled like diamonds
Then there was a room with sweets inside
Confetti floated slowly down.
It was made out of flowers
That smells like baked cakes
And rides that made the children go to sleep.
There was a room where you could
Make your own ice cream with any
Flavour you like.
You could have strawberry, chocolate
Vanilla, mint and sprinkles on top!

Sarah-Louise Killman (10)
St John's CE Primary School, Worksop

THE SECRET CAVE OF FUN

They got in and danced with laughter,
And heard sounds of chocolate water trickling down,
They started to catch all the beautiful butterflies,
They ate sweets from the trees,
And slept in candyfloss beds,
There were bouncy balls made from marshmallows
And mazes with ice cream walls
And the music played, so sweet, so subtle,
Flowing like a river in the air.

The sun shone on the chocolate water
And the children never remembered their parents again.

Gareth Anderson (10)
St John's CE Primary School, Worksop

KOPPELBERG HILL

As the mysterious man led the children
Towards the opening hillside,
He began to go slow as they drew nearer,
When inside, the mysterious man stamped his foot
And the hillside closed forever.

They swam for ages in wonderful warm water,
Whilst their parents suffered from the disastrous occurrence.
The sights were wonderful
Always sleeping on the beautiful boiling beach
Always getting delicious warm food,
Never getting older or younger
Always warm, never getting colder.
Always friends,
Having music all day
And always having sunlight.

Charlie Bartlett (10)
St John's CE Primary School, Worksop

ABROAD

When I go on holiday I get scared
Hoping that the plane doesn't crash.
Eventually we are there
To relax in the sun
And have some fun.
Explore the place
Party all night,
Lay in all you want
Until it's time to be scared again.

Sam Moore (10)
St John's CE Primary School, Worksop

My Brother

The cry of a little boy
On a dark and spooky night.
The howl of the wolf
A whinge of a boy.
A whine of a baby
Just been born
Something rattles
A baby's bottle
Pitch black
The ink of a pen dying away
Blood drips from a hanging corpse
The boy is dead, but comes alive.

Josephine Clark (11)
St John's CE Primary School, Worksop

The Magician

For the worst act he pulled a habit
out of his rat, the habbit tend under
the wable. We all chapped and cleared
and then the second act came on.
The magician got wass of glater
and made it vanish. We were all
creemed it's that bad I ate it.
My yummy took me by the hand
and we right.

Adam Marsden (11)
St John's CE Primary School, Worksop

SILENCE!

Silence is all around
It's everywhere, not even a sound,
Everything was silent amongst the trees
You couldn't even hear the gentle breeze.
I couldn't hear the plane from above
Or the sound of a graceful dove.

Everything was quiet, even space,
I think, even the human race.
I think everything was silent and gentle
If I don't hear something soon
I'm going to go *mental!*

Richard Callaghan (11)
St John's CE Primary School, Worksop

PROWLER

On a dark and spooky night
A creature began a fight,
The creature made a noise
Which frightened a load of boys.

Delicate feet walk slowly
The creature walks lowly,
The sun rises
The creature awakes,
It's a night prowler
It's a cat.

Emma Cottrell (10)
St John's CE Primary School, Worksop

DONE FLU

Done
Flu
I've joined the stew
Flea
Floor
I opened the door
Dive
Bricks
Drop some sticks
Devon
Great
I'm in a state
Fine
Hen
I'm in Big Ben
Heaven
Delve
Fig and weld
Dirteen
Lawteen
Maid's were fourteen
Big teen
Fixteen
Bigger than sixteen
Heaventeen
Late teen
Maids are inflating
Dineteen
Flempty
I went empty.

Sarah Box (11)
St John's CE Primary School, Worksop

DESERT DREAM

I drag my feet along
The soft, slightly steaming sand,
My eyes squinting,
Focusing, struggling to see where I'm going
In this vast oven.
Is that a tribe of Nomads in the distance?
My sleepiness drifts away
And I become more aware of the things around me.
But that fiery ball in the sky
Beats on
Making me feel like a roast potato.
I flick a fly from my face
And notice a flock of vultures overhead, waiting.
Caustically I drink the last few drops from my flask,
Hoping I'll last out.
I stagger on,
Curving away from a teeming tower of termites
That stands in my path.
Is that an oasis
Where I can get water and shade?
I increase my pace
And listening to the padding of my feet
Makes me feel calmed.
I arrive at the oasis
And sink into the pleasant shade.
Exhausted, I close my eyes,
The desert fades away
And I wake up in my own bedroom.

Natalie Mawson (10)
St John's CE Primary School, Worksop

MYSTICAL MEADOWS

The silent buzz of a bumblebee
Whizzing around in front of me.

The relaxing aromas of a million flowers
Fills my dreams with hope and powers.

The gentle breeze running through my hair
Makes me love all and care.

The whisper of the magical trees,
Allows all hatred and selfishness to flee.

Emma Coppin (11)
St John's CE Primary School, Worksop

THE BEAR

She leaves her den in early spring
So very hungry she'll eat anything.
Nuts, fruit, berries and fish
Mixed together
Make a great dish.

She had been tucked away all winter long,
But now she sings a different song.
Dancing and skipping all day long
Now that spring sings its song.

Rebecca Louise Wass (9)
Saville House School

MY PET

My dogs name is Teal
When I take her out she walks by my heel.

Three years old and full of life,
Fur all fluffy, brown and white.

Running, jumping and having fun,
That is what she loves to do in the sun.

The breed she is, is a springer spaniel
Searching for birds and getting in a tangle.

When she smells the vets
Her tail goes down in-between her legs.

The food she loves is lots and lots of meat,
And of course the biscuits she thinks are sweets.

When she hears a bang
She gets very frightened and runs away.

I love my dog
She is my pet.

Victoria Bowring (9)
Saville House School

SPACE

Space is dark
Space is cold
Space is where the planets are
Like Earth, Venus, Neptune and Mars
But the greatest feature of space
Is a big yellow hot sun
So, space is a great place to be.

Antonios Savva (9)
Saville House School

MY KITTEN MITZY

My kitten Mitzy is very small
She did not like my big cat at all,
She is black and white
Not heavy, but light.

Her breakfast is sweet,
She thinks it's a treat.
When it's dinner, she has tuna and salmon
Fish (yummy)
Her favourite dish,
Delish!

When she is thirsty
She never has spilled
Any of her milk
She rubs her head on the silk
Then sits on my lap.
Don't tap and ruffle her fur
Ssh! Listen to her purr.

If she is upset
Leave and let
Stroking her fur
With a soft gentle touch
Will calm her so much.

Put her out on the ground,
She will tiptoe around,
Put her in the garden
I beg your pardon.
She will run all day
In her wild west play
'What a tiring day. Hey!'

When everyone is tucked up in bed
My kitten Mitzy is hugging my ted.
When we are tucked up in bed,
All warm and nice
My kitten Mitzy is hunting for mice,
Mitzy! Play nice!

Ellalouise Whetton (10)
Saville House School

CHOCOLATE

It can be plain or milk
It is creamy and shines like silk.
It can be white or brown
It tastes good as it goes down.

It comes in many sizes and shapes
It can be cold, or warm, or baked.
It comes in different types of wrapper
At Eastertime it looks quite dapper.

I like it all the same
It gives my teeth some pain.
It isn't good for your health,
It costs a lot of your wealth.

You can eat it anywhere,
Even in bed if you dare.
Have you guessed what it is?
It's *chocolate,* it's the bizz.

Hayley Arnold (10)
Saville House School

THE SILENCE OF HOOVES

Standing in the field
All is silent and still
A sweeping breeze flies over the hill.

A rumble of thunder
The ground starts to shake
As galloping hooves approach at a tremendous rate.

He clears his nose
And paws the floor
Impatient for food he turns once more.

His nose disappears in the warm succulent grass
He gracefully moves
You don't hear him pass.

The silence of hooves is a wonderful sound
As you listen and hear
As they pound on the ground.

Natalya Baxter (10)
Saville House Schoo

TEN OUT OF TEN

When I get ten out of ten
I jump, dance and sing about
When I get ten out of ten
I run, shout and ring the bell
I'm so happy I must go and tell
Mum I got ten out of ten
'Wow!' she says 'you did well!'

Elizabeth Smith (9)
Saville House School

TOM THE BIG BLACK CAT

Tom the big black cat
Sits on his favourite mat
He sleeps most of the day
Then at night he likes to play.

He likes to sit and clean his fur
Then he smells his food and starts to purr,
Sometimes after dinner he likes to play
And even likes to catch mice in the hay.

He sits in the tree
And looks down at me.
Look, I can see the moon
Time to go in soon.

Christopher Haslam (11)
Saville House School

SPRING

I like spring
When all the people sing,
Spring brings new life
    Baby lambs
    Baby foals
Spring is a time of joy!

Spring leads into summertime,
Leaves on trees
    Colours galore
    Shining sun
I love the spring.

Matthew Davis (10)
Saville House School

DANNY THE DOLPHIN

Danny the dolphin swam through the sea
Waggling and jumping around.
I saw him perform in the sea
Entertaining you and me.
Danny the dolphin always on show
Swimming along, to and fro.
Eating fish doing tricks
Clapping, swishing with his tail he flicks.

Elliott Smith (9)
Saville House School

SNAKES

Snakes are scary
I don't know why
Slithering and twisting
Their skins are dry
Patterns and scales all over their skin
Some are fat and some are thin.

Georgio Michael (10)
Saville House School

WINTER

Winter means building up a fire,
Winter means having load of soup in bed
Winter means animals hibernate
Winter means Santa Claus
Laughs on Christmas Day.

Harriett Hawkins (5)
Saville House School

The Wind

The wind was strong
So very strong
But one day the wind
Swapped with the sun.
'I am not strong anymore,' said the wind,
So the wind left the sun to shine
On the man.

Next day the wind wasn't very happy
Because the sun was so happy.
Shining up there, shining down on the people,
So the wind swapped the sun in the night
The next morning, the sun wasn't very happy
But up there the wind swaying happily,
Was even happier than before.
Because he was up there with his windy friends.

Fiona Redfern (9)
Saville House School

My Colourful Bluebird

My colourful bluebird sat on her nest,
With seven blue eggs beneath her breast.
She is blue and very small
And only eats bread and nothing else at all.

Hopping, tweeting, chirping all day,
Smiling in a bird's special way.
Looking for worms underground,
But there is none to be found.

Gabbrielle Williams (9)
Saville House School

PRESENTS

I love presents
I ask my mum and dad
But when it's someone else's birthday
I go mad.

I've got a pair of shoes that's all I've got
But I told my mum and dad
I want a lot.

Ingela Khan (9)
Saville House School

BOOKS

Books are great
They're my best mate,
Books have lots of fantasies
Just for me and my friends.

I like pirate books
Because they've got those nasty hooks
I also like dinner books
Because they tell you how to cook.

Jack Thrall (9)
Saville House School

REMEMBER

Remember, remember the 5th of November,
The bonfire crackles, fireworks pop,
Catherine wheels whiz, rockets bang!
Sparklers hiss, the smell of toffee apple and bonfire,
Toffee burning, hot dogs too.

Rebecca McGeorge (8)
Woodsetts Primary School

TIGER'S AWAY!

Carted away from my perfect home,
My claws held down by bricks,
Nothing for me to do,
I've been thrown into a world
That I think is new.
Then I hear someone say,
'Lower the beast in today',
Everyone thinks I'm mean
And vicious,
But the truth is I'm calm and
Peaceful.

My cage is locked,
There's no coming out,
Then the ringmaster comes to see,
Gets out his whip and starts
Whipping me.
I'm all sad and lonely,
Wish I was home playing
Locally.
Now I've got to learn to train,
Facing all that terrible pain,
Never seeing the jungle again.

Lucy Potts (9)
Woodsetts Primary School

ONE BY ONE

One by one,
One by one,
Waves are prancing,
Then they're gone.

Emma Tweed (6)
Woodsetts Primary School

READING RECORDS

Reading records,
Waste of time!
Reading records,
I'll never do it in my own time!

Reading records,
Hate a lot!
Reading records,
Bad plot!

Reading records,
Pen to paper,
Reading records,
I'll do it later!

Reading records,
Waste of space,
Reading records,
Get in my face!

Jack Bowler (9)
Woodsetts Primary School

CREEPING

Spinning a web in the dark night,
Frost eaten away as the dark night draws to an end,
The spiders scuttle around to try and find
A damp place, leaving their web alone
When the prey lands on its web,
Instantly he spots it and draws closer and closer.

Laura Wilson (11)
Woodsetts Primary School

BONFIRE NIGHT

On bonfire night,
The stars are bright,
The people look at the guy
Then I go and buy
A hot dog,
The fire works zoom and boom
Then I watch the guy burning,
Bang, crackle,
Then there's drinks
And fireworks bring
Light to the sky.
They fly very high
Next to the stars,
Then the stars go all colours,
The fire goes hiss
And then all of the adults,
Buy their children a sparkler
And then go home to bed.

Stacy Wilkinson (8)
Woodsetts Primary School

SUMMER'S FUN

Summer's fun, summer's fun,
Summer's fun for everyone,
Boys and girls laugh and play
All through the lovely summer days.

Summer's fun, summer's fun,
Summer's fun for everyone,
Skipping ropes leave the ground,
While children jump up and down.

Emma Longmore (8)
Woodsetts Primary School

BONFIRE NIGHT!

Stars so bright,
Fireworks go bang!
In the middle of the night,
Burgers sizzle in the night,
Catherine wheels whiz round,
Making a sssshhhh sound,
Rockets zoom up into the sky,
People stare at the colours in the sky,
As the fireworks say goodnight,
People watch Guy Fawkes swivel down
But that isn't the end of the fireworks,
Zoom Catherine wheels,
Rockets, fireworks, Roman candles,
Explode boom! Bang! Crash!
Everyone says oooohhh aahhh.

Laura Lacey (8)
Woodsetts Primary School

SPIDERS

Creeping crawling across the ground,
Waiting for its prey to come around,
Spiders are all sizes, big and small,
Some creep, some crawl.

Spin their webs in the trees,
I just saw one, it had very wobbly knees,
I wonder how many bones spiders have,
Here come some others, fab!

Emma Dixon (11)
Woodsetts Primary School

I Don't Like Spiders

I don't like spiders,
They creep, crawl,
Scatter on the wall.

I don't like spiders,
Big ones, small ones, lounging around,
Picking up your clothes, spiders being found.

I don't like spiders,
They make me screech and whine,
Crawling in that perfect line.

I don't like spiders,
Little bodies, big long legs,
In a dark corner, they lay their eggs.

Belinda Hall (11)
Woodsetts Primary School

Bonfire Night

Bonfire Night stars are bright,
Rockets whiz, sparklers fizz,
Baked potatoes sizzling on the plate,
Toffee apples good to chew,
Lots of fun for me and you,
Fireworks zoom, hiss and bang,
Cascading stars go drifting by,
Rainbow colours come down from the sky,
Sizzling sausages - please be mine,
Golden rain stuck on the pane of my window.

Charlotte Phelps (7)
Woodsetts Primary School

SPIDERS

Spiders creeping around the garden,
Crawling up the wall,
Making sure that nobody steps on them at all!
Spiders are secretive and hide nothing but fear,
When some people see them, they shed loads of tears.

With hair on their legs and hair on their body,
With eyes which spook you out,
They're lifeless and still when they come in front of you,
So take my advice,
Just run off!
Spiders creeping around the garden,
Crawling up the wall,
Making sure that nobody steps on them at all!

Hester Dickinson (11)
Woodsetts Primary School

ARNIE

Arnie is the fattest cat,
Gobbling all the food,
He eats all day,
He eats all night,
He gives you such a fright!
When he goes outside,
He slides down the slide,
He's such a clown,
He would bounce up and down.
I love little Arnie
And so does the
Rest of the family.

Holly Kisby (8)
Woodsetts Primary School

SPIDER

S ecretly creeping in the garden,
P rowling around the empty pots,
I n broken plaster on the floor,
D amp and dark inside a bush,
E ating flies and bits of bugs,
R avaging through a dreary corner,
S earching for a place to stay.

S piders scary, furry legs,
P ouncing round their sticky web,
I nching up the gutter pipe,
D aringly falling in the bath,
E ggs in a sack, all white and sticky,
R unning round the garden wall.

Rosie Kisby (10)
Woodsetts Primary School

A FUNNY DAY

I'm not sure what to say,
So I think I will put it this way.
It happened one day,
It was in the month of May.
We went to Ikea,
For what I've no idea.
On the way back,
We stopped for a snack and had
Octopus and chips for dinner!
When we got home it got even worse
Because someone had pinched my mum's
Purse, oh dear, oh dear.

Gabriella Renzi (8)
Woodsetts Primary School

READING

Reading's cool,
Reading's great,
But you can't do it,
If you're late, late, late.

My favourite books are mystic,
Cos they have dragons, knights
And things that make a fright
And I like ghosts that come
Out at dark, dark nights.

Reading's cool!
Reading's great,
But you can't do it,
If you're late, late, late.

Joe McLoughlin (8)
Woodsetts Primary School

MY DAD

My dad is mad,
My dad is good,
My dad is going out,
My dad is walking home,
My dad is happy,
My dad is going to work,
My dad is at home,
My dad is going golfing,
My dad is getting his coat on,
My dad is bad,
My dad is going upstairs.

Adam Vine (7)
Woodsetts Primary School

SPIDER

S   piders crawl,
P   rickle the floor,
I   n the plant pot,
D   own the drain,
E   ven outside in the rain,
R   ising higher and higher,
S   ome day he'll be up Ecclesfield Prire!

S   preading lace,
P   laying in grace,
I   n the web, comes a fly,
D   rinks the blood until it's dry,
E   very day he gets the same,
R   ainy days end in shame,
S   piders live a life of fame.

Christopher Pickering (11)
Woodsetts Primary School

FIREWORKS

Fireworks crackle,
Fireworks bang,
Fireworks roar,
Fireworks zoom,
Fireworks hiss,
Fireworks whiz,
Fireworks bang,
Catherine wheel goes
Round, round and round.

Oliver Leary (8)
Woodsetts Primary School

SCHOOL

School's fun,
School's fun,
Everyone lets us play and run,

School's nice,
School's nice
And we eat a lot of rice.

School's cool,
School's cool
And there is a big rule.

School's great,
School's great
And that's what I think.

Amy Oakley (9)
Woodsetts Primary School

MY CAT

My cat Fluffy is grey and white,
I don't mind her when she purrs at night,
She bites a lot, scratches too,
I love her and she loves me too.
There's one problem with my cat Fluffy,
Dogs is the problem with my cat Fluffy,
Dogs, dogs, dogs, there's always a dog,
Inside or out, they'll be a dog,
I'm always scared when there's a dog,
I bring my cat in when there's a dog.

Lauren Smith (7)
Woodsetts Primary School

SPIDER, SPIDER ON MY GARDEN WALL

The spider finds a perfect place,
To spin her web of silk and lace,
My garden wall is the best
Place for her to build her nest.
Her first big catch is a bluebottle fly,
So she spins him up and sucks him dry.
Other victims fly into the trap,
Oh, they try so hard to flip and flap,
So, next time you see a spider please beware,
Cos if you don't you're in for a scare.

Matthew Maloney (10)
Woodsetts Primary School

NIGHT

It was night,
I switched on the light,
I saw a star,
What was far,
I saw the sky,
What was dry and powdery blue
Just like you.
I went to the beach and had a feast
And went back and had a snack.

Ben Armstrong (6)
Woodsetts Primary School

FIREWORKS

Fireworks soaring, sizzling, sparkling,
Lighting the night,
Catherine wheel spinning round and round,
This way, that way.
Rockets blasting in the air, lighting the night sky,
Fireworks sizzling, sparkling this way, that way,
Round and round, falling silently to the ground.

Thomas Jarvis (8)
Woodsetts Primary School

FIREWORKS

Fireworks sparkle,
Fireworks fly,
Fireworks set off into the sky,
The bonfire burns angry red,
All the people then go to bed.

Mathew Hall (8)
Woodsetts Primary School

THREE BY THREE

Three by three,
Three by three,
I kiss my
Mum and dad
And they kiss me.

Laura Tweed (5)
Woodsetts Primary School

SPIDERS

Anxious spider spinning a web,
Going to catch his prey,
In the cold wet rain, he toddles around the garden,
In a flash and a light, he's finished,
Waiting in a tree, he spots a fly in his web,
Then creeps up and pounces up on to the fly.

Kirsty Waterhouse (10)
Woodsetts Primary School

WEBS OF SPIDERS

I wait, till one spider comes to watch
It spin its web,
Some people would think they're creepy
I think they're fascinating.
The way it goes around, around and around.
A fly comes, it sticks to the web,
It pounces on its prey, it dies.

Matthew Hobbs (10)
Woodsetts Primary School

SPIDERS

S ecretive spiders slowly,
P acing up and down my garden,
I n the sunlight making silly webs,
D ancing in the long, brown grass,
'E ek' cries my friend, she doesn't like them,
R avaging through the dusty leaves,
S piders legs tickle on my arm, they won't do you any harm.

Olivia Liversidge (10)
Woodsetts Primary School